Y0-EDU-323

FAITH. FOCUS. ACTION.

The Journey to BECOMING WHO YOU ARE

"Success is created from the inside out!
Learn who you are, what you want,
and develop the courage to fight for it!"
~Chereace A. Richards

Chereace A. Richards

Gail -
Celebrate the
Possibilities!
Chereace R.

Copyright © 2013 Chereace A. Richards
First Edition
All rights reserved.

No part of this publication may be reproduced, stored in a retrieval system or transmitted in any form or by any means, electronic, mechanical, photocopying, recording, scanning or otherwise, except under the terms of the Copyright, Designs and Patents Act 1988 or under the terms of a license issued by the Copyright Licensing Agency Ltd.

Legal Disclaimer

The Publisher and the Authors make no representations or warranties with respect to the accuracy or completeness of the contents of this work and specifically disclaim all warranties, including without limitation warranties of fitness for a particular purpose. No warranty maybe created or extended by sales or promotional materials. The advice and strategies contained herein may not be suitable for every situation.

Neither the publishers nor the authors shall be liable for damages arising herefrom. The fact that an organization or website is referred to in this work as a citation and/or a potential source of further information does not mean that the author or the publisher endorses the information the organization or website it may provide or recommendations it may make.

Further, readers should be aware that Internet websites listed in this work may have changed or disappeared between when this work was written and when it is read.

For booking and more information on Chereace A. Richards, go to www.chereacerichards.com

ISBN-10: 1620304465
ISBN-13: 9781620304464

Table of Contents

This book is dedicated to all of the women who inspire me every day to be, do, and have more.

ACKNOWLEDGMENTS

I want to acknowledge the individuals who have inspired me to begin my journey to becoming and encouraged me to never give up. I thank my Lord and Savior Jesus for never giving up on me and allowing Your will in my life to shine! I praise You and promise to serve you with my life! I honor my husband, Stanley, for loving me unconditionally. Thank you for always seeing the best in me. It's because of your love, support, encouragement, and belief that I am able to do what I do and be who I am. I love you and thank God for bringing you into my life. I want to thank my sons, Stanley, Jr. and Isaiah, for challenging me every day to be a better parent and a better person. I do what I do for you! Thank you to my mom, father, step-dad, and sisters for loving me in spite of me! Your constant love and support has always been a source of comfort for me, as I know that I always have a safe place to just be! I will always love you! I thank the 5LINX Co-Founders for creating an amazing opportunity for me—this ordinary person—to live this extraordinary life. I am forever grateful. I thank the 5LINX family for loving and embracing me. Our collective journey to becoming and having all that God has for us is a source of inspiration for me. I am excited about our movement to change lives one person at a time. Lastly, to my brother-in-law, Tim Richards, your faith has inspired me! Thank you.

PREFACE

Life is a marathon! I never knew how important my marathon experiences would become until they taught me some very important lessons that I used to change the direction of my life.

With God's help, I managed to find the strength I needed to take an active role in my own destiny, something I think women often overlook in their lives.

There was a pivotal moment for me during Bible study one evening, when I came across a scripture I had read before, but never truly considered. It was from 2 Timothy 1:7:

"God has not given us a spirit of fear; but of power, love, and a sound mind."

These powerful words struck a chord with me, and I thought about the first time I entertained the idea of completing a marathon race. I wasn't a very fit person, so it would be a significant challenge—but to this day I have never felt something as rewarding as crossing that finish line.

In the beginning I was full of fear, and had no idea where to begin. I eventually signed up with a local training program that was preparing individuals for this type of event, and they taught me what I needed to eat, and how to discipline myself for the coming race.

When I read that scripture I realized what a profound impact my marathon training and experience had played in my life. I felt empowered and inspired—and I began to change the way I perceived my abilities, my limitations, and myself.

God doesn't want us to lead unfulfilled lives of stress and worry. Yet that's the path I had chosen for myself, and I see many other women doing the same. You refuse to stand up and seize control of your career and your future, and as a result—you never get to experience that 'marathon' moment as I did.

I finally realized that I could do anything, and that God wanted me to be more than what I had allowed myself to become. If you take a closer look at that scripture, you'll see truth in those words. God didn't design us to be scared of our potential, or to hide away from the incredible things that we are able to do—the world made us that way.

Instead, we were created to be able to do incredible things, if only we had access to the self-discipline, love, and inner power that the scripture speaks about. And so for me, life is like a marathon. Some of us choose to be spectators and remain on the sidelines of life.

A few of us choose to really get involved and become a runner in the marathon of life. It's these people who are able to truly experience what life is all about. A spectator couldn't possibly know the will that is required on that last stretch of tarmac.

You need to join the race, and to learn how to win it. That's what God always intended for you. And that's why I've written *FAITH, FOCUS, ACTION,* so that you can have that 'marathon' moment, and realize that there is so much more out there, you just need to reach out and take it. All you need is within you now!

This book is designed to empower and encourage women to be all that they were put on this earth to be. As women, we have the ability to accomplish amazing things in our lifetime. No matter what our background or upbringing, we can strive toward the best that life has to offer.

Powerful women in politics, entertainment, and business have started out from humble beginnings only to find themselves on historical climbs to great heights. Do you think Michelle Obama, Oprah and Beyoncé, just to name a few successful women, knew what the outcome would be when their struggles were met with opposition and defeat? No. With determination, dedication, and commitment, they persevered and went on to find success on many levels. They believed in their vision, worked very hard, and took advantage of the opportunities they were given. When the time was right, they were able to reap the benefits.

As the Roman philosopher Seneca said, "Luck is what happens when opportunity meets preparation." It takes a deep belief in your abilities, a lot of hard work, and a sense of stick-to-itiveness to make things happen. I believe that faith, focus, and action are the winning combination that can make it all transpire—can make your dreams a reality.

Let's begin the journey of becoming who you are destined to become…with faith, focus, and action!

INTRODUCTION

In 1999 and 2000, I ran two marathons. At the time of writing this book, I will have completed my third marathon—the 37th Marine Corps Marathon. Prior to those years, I hadn't run a day in my life. Initially, I was intimidated at the thought of running 26.2 miles. I wasn't unfamiliar with this feeling—it was the same thing I felt whenever I started something new, whether it was starting a new job, becoming a mother for the first time, or starting a new business. In the same way, running was intimidating because it was new and unknown to me. I didn't know what to expect.

My guess is that I am not alone when facing new challenges. We can all relate to those fears associated with starting something different. The key is to not let our fear of the unknown stop us dead in our tracks, and to fight through these feelings that may paralyze us and cause us to question and second-guess ourselves. This thought process, when left unchecked, causes so many people to miss out on the opportunities that may lead them ever closer to achieving their dreams.

My marathon preparation taught me so much about my life and what I could accomplish when I put my mind to it. I asked myself some questions. Why do we so often give up on our dreams? Why do we limit ourselves by what we believe we can do? Why don't we challenge ourselves to do more, be more, and have more?

This book seeks to help you answer these questions. I want you, dear reader, to find out what, if anything, is holding you back from identifying and fulfilling your purpose. I want to equip you with the strategies and techniques you can use to empower you.

I chose the analogy of a marathon because I believe it is a great metaphor for going the distance with your dreams. Marathons are not run quickly; they take time and dedication to complete. Just like discovering a life that is rewarding, significant, and full of purpose takes time and is worth all of the effort. When you are in step with God's will, have the right motivation, and are willing to work hard, you can achieve your dreams.

Ladies, the time has come to thrive, not just survive!

CHAPTER 1

Start Where You Are

"A journey of a thousand miles begins with a single step."

This quote from the Chinese philosopher Lao-tzu is commonly translated to mean that no journey can start without taking that first step, no matter how small. While that is true, rather than emphasizing the first step, Lao-tzu regarded action as something that arises naturally from stillness. Another potential phrasing that could be interpreted from the original Chinese would be that even the longest journey must begin where you stand.

Prior to signing up for my first marathon in 1999, I had not run a single mile. In fact, friends and family would tell you that I didn't particularly care for running or exercise, in general. However, I am the type of person who likes a challenge—who needs to set a goal and reach for it. I decided to enroll in a local training program in an effort to reach some weight loss goals I had set. I must admit that at the time, my only thought was that training for a marathon might help me lose the weight. I had not given much thought to the reality of running 26.2 miles in a row!

That is why I encourage you to get started on whatever your goals are right now. It doesn't have to be a perfect start, with everything just so. Remember, this is just the beginning and you can't reach your goal until you take that initial step. If I had let the reality of training for a marathon keep me from signing up for the class, I would never have run a marathon, let alone three. The same is true for you in your life. Don't let your past define what you can do in your future. You have to start where you are.

Oswald Chambers says that, "Faith is deliberate confidence in the character of God whose ways you may not understand at the time." You may not know what the future holds, but when you know who holds your future it makes it easier to start where you are. Taking the first step in any endeavor can be intimidating and challenging. Imagine taking that step with the belief that wherever you are, God will meet you there. Having faith allows me to move confidently in the direction God shows me. Did I know on the day I signed up for that training program, that I would eventually become a runner—even learning to love running just for the fun of it? No, but I did know that God was calling me to action. I knew that I wanted to lose weight and God put that opportunity in front of me. My only responsibility was to step out in faith and enroll in the program.

Martin Luther King, Jr. is quoted as saying, "Faith is taking the first step even when you can't see the whole staircase." In essence, what this means is we can take the first step, assuming the rest will be there. Even if we have doubts and fears, as long as we keep going, we will arrive. Like Dr. King, we all have the ability to embark on a journey of a thousand miles when we tap into the divine power within us.

This faith can give us the courage to face any uncertainties of the future. Faith will give our tired feet new strength as we continue to move forward. During those times when our days become dreary and our nights become dark, faith will see us through. Each of us has the power of faith and we can utilize that power to create a meaningful and abundant life. Like Dr. King, you can take "the first step even when you can't see the whole staircase." For me, exercising my faith keeps me going even when I don't want to. It keeps me moving forward, even when I am afraid or overwhelmed.

Joel Osteen writes, "Dreams only come true when the dreamer takes action." You may not even be aware of what the dream will lead to. In those moments, ask God to give you wisdom and clarity. Maybe you are having a hard time holding onto it because of the pressures of life. Or maybe you've been waiting and this is your moment to step out and move forward in faith.

No dream can come true if you don't believe and take action. If you can conceive and believe, you can achieve. Our biggest ideas and greatest dreams must compel us into motion. When we take that first step, God will take two. It might not even be in the direction that we envisioned when we set out. God needs us to start moving first. So many people sit on their ideas, mulling them over in their heads. At some point you have to take action and move out with a sense of purpose. My initial goal was to lose weight; however, I stuck with the program and now run most days. And I enjoy it! Most significantly, that step was the catalyst to my believing that I could achieve any goal I had set for myself. It transformed my faith and empowered me to reach new levels in my life!

The true goal of life is to do the best you can with what you have at every moment. Jim Elliot once said, "Wherever you are—be all there." Make it your ambition to live out your gifts and talents to the fullest.

Questions for Reflection

What are some goals you want to achieve? Write down your top three goals.

What is a first step that you can take today, towards any of your goals? Don't worry about the process or the end result (remember, you may not know yet what the end result will be!). Focus instead on what the first step looks like.

Don't let your past define your future. List three things you have already accomplished that you did not think you ever would. If you did it before, you have what it takes to do it again.

"The first step towards getting somewhere is to decide that you are not going to stay where you are."

~John Pierpont Morgan

"What we call the beginning is often the end. And to make an end is to make a beginning. The end is where we start from."

~T.S. Eliot

"Take the first step, and your mind will mobilize all its forces to your aid. But the first essential is that you begin. Once the battle is started, all that is within and without you will come to your assistance."

~Robert Collier

CHAPTER 2

Don't Lose Hope

Oprah Winfrey is quoted as saying, "You are worthy because you were born." Statistics show that while on average about 200 out of 500 million sperm cells survive the journey to the egg, ultimately only one sperm made its way to the egg in order to create you. That is no accident. You are meant to be right here right now.

In scripture it is written, "For you created my inmost being; you knit me together in my mother's womb. I praise you because I am fearfully and wonderfully made; your works are wonderful, I know that full well. My frame was not hidden from you when I was made in the secret place, when I was woven together in the depths of the earth. Your eyes saw my unformed body; all the days ordained for me were written in your book before one of them came to be." Psalm 139:13-16

Long before you were born, God knew you. He knew your name, what you would look like, where you would live, and more. God knew it all. He knew what plans He had for you and what gifts He would bestow upon you. Because you were born and are here right now is reason to celebrate! From the beginning of time, there is a purpose for every creature ever created. God does not make mistakes. It doesn't matter how you got here—planned or unplanned, the fact that you were born means something. You were created for a unique purpose in life. You and only you can fulfill that purpose. No one else on this earth can do what God created for you to do.

Our job, if you will, is to learn why God created us. I once heard a speaker say that there are two important days in our life: 1) the day we were born and 2) the day we know why we were born. I believe that as soon as we tap into our God-given purpose, we can begin to live life to its fullest potential. You can begin to live your purpose out. It is then that you can experience true fulfillment, joy, and peace. You will then be living an authentic life.

So, take a moment to ask yourself these simple questions: Now that I am here, why am I here? What purpose in God's plan am I here to fulfill? Ask yourself, who am I really?

When I realized that God knew me before I was born, I stood in awe before Him. It brought me such joy and excitement to know that God thought of me in that fashion. It gave me hope to know that there is a greater plan and that I am a part of it. Don't lose hope—know that you are a part of His plan, too.

Mike Ditka famously said, "Before you can win, you have to believe you are worthy." Know that as a child of God, you are worthy. I believe that success in any area of your life begins with self-belief and the knowledge that you deserve all that God has for you.

We all know the saying, "Idle hands are the devil's playground." That is not true. You can be busy working and creating wonderful things with your hands, but where is your mind? What are your thoughts centered on? For this reason, I believe it should be, "An idle mind is the devil's playground." An idle mind is an undisciplined mind, a wondering mind. As Christians, we need to be disciplined in every aspect of our lives. It is not enough to just control our actions, though that does take a lot of strength. The real battle is in the mind; for it is our thoughts and our mind that ultimately control our actions. Without a change of mind, your outward conformity will fail. As it says in Psalms 1:1-5,

"Blessed is the man
who walks not in the counsel of the wicked,
nor stands in the way of sinners,
nor sits in the seat of scoffers;
but his delight is in the law of the LORD,
and on his law he meditates day and night.

"He is like a tree
planted by streams of water
that yields its fruit in its season,
and its leaf does not wither.
In all that he does, he prospers. The wicked are not so,
but are like chaff that the wind drives away.

"Therefore the wicked will not stand in the judgment,
nor sinners in the congregation of the righteous;
for the LORD knows the way of the righteous,
but the way of the wicked will perish."

The man who meditates on the Law of the Lord is like a tree planted by rivers of water. This person is alive, thriving, strong, and mighty. We need to take our thoughts captive and replace them with the Word of God. We need to condition our minds to respond Godly during times of adversity rather than dive into self-pity, rage, and impatience, which all are worldly.

Philippians 4:8 states, "Finally, brothers, whatever is true, whatever is noble, whatever is right, whatever is pure, whatever is lovely, whatever is admirable—if anything is excellent or praiseworthy—think about such things." We all have negative and positive thoughts that compete within our minds. Every minute, every second of every day these thoughts conflict and engage in battle within us! Philippians 4:8 tells us exactly what types of things we need to be thinking about. My pastor always says, "We have to take every thought captive." By doing so, we choose to focus on the things that are positive and that bring us hope. Those negative thoughts and untruths that do not serve us must be discarded. The negative thoughts are not of God.

So how do you keep hope alive? How do you wrestle the bad thoughts to the ground? You pray and meditate on God's word and believe in yourself. Remember that God created you for a specific purpose and has equipped you with all that you need in order to make His plans for your life a reality. Meditate on the knowledge that you are His handiwork, His majesty.

I believe that having faith is a huge part of winning in life. For me, faith means believing that God is going to do what He says He will do. Even if current circumstances don't necessarily show it, I still believe it and this gives me hope. Furthermore, it means trusting God during the good times, as well as the bad times. It's during our toughest times that our faith is strengthened.

Having faith allows me to move confidently in the direction that God has shown me. It keeps me moving forward even when I am full of doubt and afraid. Faith gives me a sense of peace, knowing that God will not leave me nor forsake me. I haven't always been this strong in my faith, however.

I remember the year 2002 very clearly. I was married, working, a new homeowner, and the mother of a brand-new baby. The rug was pulled out from under me when I was let go from work. When I lost my job, my faith was shaken to the core. I lost confidence in myself and even questioned why God would allow this to happen to me. I worried about our survival. Things only got worse when my aggressive search for a job produced nothing. For months on end, I didn't get any responses from the hundreds of résumés I sent out. I became depressed, giving into feelings of worry and anxiety. I began to give credence to those negative thoughts in my head that the reason I had lost my job, and wasn't getting any new offers, was that I wasn't worthy. I began to doubt my abilities and felt that perhaps my skills were no longer desirable. In looking back, I can say that this was Satan's way of trying to keep me down. Once I understood this, I was able to snap out of my funk…and land a new job with a higher salary.

In John 10:10, the Bible states that Satan is the thief, who comes only to steal and kill and destroy. It is for that reason Jesus has come so that we may have life and have it to the full.

Satan will use whatever he can in our lives to attack our faith and create doubt in God. Therefore it is important for us to be aware of his tactics and how he will use them on us. We must acknowledge that Satan does operate in our lives and tries to keep us in bondage. It is with this knowledge that we can prepare ourselves to fight him off when he tries to attack. That is the conclusion I came to in 2002 and it is the same way I feel today, many years later.

Questions for Reflection

Take this page to write out what you think your purpose is in life. This may change and evolve as you move forward, but for this moment, write something. Acknowledge that you have a God-given purpose in this life. This will serve as the first step in your journey to leading a fulfilled life.

Journal some ways that Satan has tried to keep you in bondage. Maybe you are in the midst of a spiritual warfare at this moment. Take the time to write it down. Study what you wrote and look for patterns or other areas in your life where he has manipulated your thoughts and actions in a similar way. Once you know better, you can do better.

"He who has faith has...an inward reservoir of courage, hope, confidence, calmness, and assuring trust that all will come out well—even though to the world it may appear to come out most badly."

~B. C. Forbes

"Never talk defeat. Use words like hope, belief, faith, victory."

~Norman Vincent Peale

"If you lose hope, somehow you lose the vitality that keeps life moving, you lose that courage to be, that quality that helps you go on in spite of it all."

~Martin Luther King, Jr.

CHAPTER 3

Encourage Yourself

You may have seen the movie *Invictus*. It is based on the life of Nelson Mandela and covers the tumultuous time after he became President of South Africa. In an effort to unite the country, Mandela takes advantage of an opportunity he sees with the game of rugby. As South Africa was about to host the Rugby World Cup, he pushed the South African team to travel all over the country, promoting the sport. Nelson tells the captain of the team, "We need inspiration…because in order to build our nation, we must exceed our own expectations." The team that was expected to make the quarterfinals at best went on to win the World Cup. Along the way, they beat much stronger competitors, united a fractious country, and truly did exceed their own expectations. There are times in life when we must encourage ourselves in order to exceed our own expectations.

By nature, I am a shy and introverted person. I am not the loudest person in the room, nor will I ever be. I tend to be analytical and make decisions based on facts rather than emotions. My desire to always maintain control means that I am methodical in my decision-making and actions. For years, I viewed this aspect of my personality as a negative. As a result, I limited myself from taking risks because I was afraid I didn't have the "right stuff." When I compared myself to others who took bigger risks, were more outgoing, and seemed to fill a room with flamboyant personality—I felt I came up short.

What a mistake that was! That kind of thinking is self-defeating. By thinking so little of myself, I was limiting what I could accomplish. Venus Williams says, "You have to believe in yourself when no one else does—that makes you a winner right there." If I didn't believe I was capable of being a winner in the big leagues of life, who would? I thought I didn't have the right qualities to succeed. This leads me to ask the question, "What are the right qualities?" If we believe that God created each of us with a unique purpose, then that should be enough to encourage us that we are all winners. Regardless of what we convince ourselves of—or what others tell us about ourselves—we are champions because we are children of God. If all we do is seek to become all that God has called us to be, we will be victorious in life.

Donald Trump says, "As long as you're going to be thinking anyway, think big." I would certainly not have been accused of thinking big! In fact, I had been limiting my actions to mimic how I felt about myself. This began to change when I focused on encouraging myself with positive thinking. For so many years I played it safe. Decisions I made in life were based on others' and my own limited belief in what I was capable of. I did not think it was possible to do anything in life other than to play it safe. Playing it safe is similar to thinking small, in my view. I conformed to outside influences and fell victim to my own fears and doubts. Ultimately, I found myself stuck between being afraid of success and fearing failure at the same time. These internal struggles kept me stuck in an endless loop of feeling unfulfilled. Deep down inside, I knew that I was capable of more and I certainly wanted more for my life. I didn't know where to start on putting my heart's desire into action.

I began to educate myself on the power of positive thinking. I believe in a simple equation: education + process = transformation/results. I realized that if I wanted a different result, I was going to have to change the input. I began reading personal development books. The book entitled *Think and Grow Rich* by Napoleon Hill was one such book. This book helped begin to shape my attitudes and beliefs about entrepreneurship and what might be possible for me. I attended workshops and seminars that gave me strategies and techniques. I applied these tips to change my habits of belief in myself.

I once heard Marshall Sylver say, "Those who think govern those who labor." How could I use this information to change the path I was on? By beginning with the way I thought about my abilities and myself. A Tony Robbins seminar, Unleash the Power Within, confirmed what I had already begun seeing. I was trapped in a limited story. What I mean by story is the meaning we all give to the things that happen in our lives. During our lifetime, things are going to happen; and what I have learned is that nothing has meaning except the meaning that I give it. So, instead of giving a disempowering meaning, I choose an empowering meaning to life events; a meaning that encourages me and moves me forward. This meaning infuses every decision and has a ripple effect on your life. In my case, my belief in my story (that I was too shy or not flamboyant enough) was limiting my potential.

What I soon discovered is that I had a choice as to how I could let this story affect my life. We all have a choice. Because our actions are directly influenced by the choices we make, I needed to put my controlling tendencies to good use! I changed my perspective and quit seeing my personality as negative or disempowered. Instead, whenever I became conscious that I was giving into a negative thought, I dismissed it, or, I changed it into a positive and empowering thought. I learned how to dismiss thoughts that didn't serve or move me forward on my journey. This took a lot of practice and still does. Satan is busy fighting for precious territory inside our minds. This is how we allow ourselves to keep from thinking small.

What helped me the most along the way is strengthening my relationship with God. In addition to attending worship services on a regular basis, I became involved in several ministries within the church. The Divine Discipleship for Sisters (DDS) changed my life completely. Through this ministry, I learned how to spend time with God in order to develop an intimate relationship with Him. As I drew closer to God, He began to show me the meaning of the verse from Philippians 4:13, "I can do all things through Christ who strengthens me." If you just read the first part of this verse, it might strike you as a boast of self: "I can do all things." This is the spirit that causes many to stumble and fall because they rely solely on their power. Many feel that it is by their own might and power that they succeed.

But the next two words in the verse take this out of the context of arrogance altogether: "through Christ." It is not an immodest brag. It is that I can do all things through Christ! There is a huge difference. It is one thing for someone to say, "I can do all things." It is very different to confess, "I can do all things through Christ."

To get the impact of this, stop and think about what you can't do without Him! Without Him, you could not have sufficient knowledge of God and His power to do more than you could ever think or imagine. He has the power to promote you and position you to live an inspired life full of joy, peace, and happiness. So with Christ, and in our relationship of active faith in Him, we have strength we could not have any other way. We have the strength to overcome and to be, to do, and to have more out of life. I realize that I am not alone on this journey. My Lord and Savior Jesus Christ is with me and through the power of the Holy Spirit I can do what He has called me to do. I can live big, bold, and on purpose! That very same life-affirming power is available to you, as well.

Have you ever imagined that you were blind? I have tried many times to identify with those who are blind by taking just a few steps with my eyes closed. After a couple of steps, I am completely disoriented. It is so unnatural for us to walk without looking and knowing where we are going, yet that is precisely what Paul says we Christians must do in 2 Corinthians 5:7, "For we walk by faith, not by sight." Those who "walk by sight" depend on their senses for direction. They rely on what they see, hear and feel. But what if you feel you are surrounded by negative feedback—both from others and from inside yourself? What if these undesirable thoughts are keeping you from reaching your greatest potential, as divined by God?

Those who "walk by faith" entrust in the Lord for direction. They rely on the Word of God for clarity and walk in great expectation that the best is yet to come. In 2008, I exercised walking by faith in a major way. I was at a crossroads in my life and I had to make a vital decision—return to a job after an eight-week leave, or resign to pursue my business full time. I was afraid to give up the security of a stable job; a job that offered a good salary and benefits. But something was calling to me and I felt that it was the right time for me to move on. My mind had been conditioned to maintain the status quo. The thought of trading job security for the unknown had me in a constant state of worry, fear, and confusion.

During this time, on a Saturday night, I prayed fervently for direction and clarity. The next day, a Sunday, we went to our church for worship. Imagine my surprise when the title of the sermon was, "Which way do we go from here?" The main point of the sermon was that in life, we basically always have three choices:

1. We can stay where we are.
2. We can move backward.
3. We can move forward.

The message ended with the reminder that our destiny is always ahead of us. God had answered my prayer. I knew without a doubt that I was supposed to walk away from my job, build my business full time, and embrace His purpose for me. God's purpose for me was not to stay in the job, but to take a leap of faith and trust Him. I felt so many emotions that morning—all of them were good. Fear, worry, and doubt were replaced with excitement, joy, and most importantly, peace. *I still did not know what my future held, but I knew who held my future.* Armed with that knowledge, I gave my resignation the next day. To God be the glory because my last day of employment was April 11, 2008, and I haven't look back since! Every day I am moving forward in the purpose God has for my life. There comes a time when you have to take a leap of faith and grow wings along the way. It is during these times that we see how powerful we are, through Christ Jesus.

Questions for Reflection

Take a moment to reflect and come up with how you would define yourself. What terms come to mind when you imagine describing yourself to someone else?

Now take any words that would be considered negative out of your list and re-imagine them in a positive frame or light (for example, my tendency to be controlling could be seen as leadership). This exercise is an illustration of how the gifts we have been given may need to be channeled in a new direction!

People often miss out on reaching their goals not because they aimed too high and fell short, but because they aimed too low and hit the mark. Write down some of the BIG dreams you have—the sky's the limit!

Now, what are the stories have you convinced yourself of that are keeping you from reaching for those big dreams? Write those stories down and begin the process of transformation by turning the negative stories in your life into empowering statements!

"And no, we don't know where it will lead. We just know that there's something much bigger than any of us here."

~Steve Jobs

"Twenty years from now, you will be more disappointed by the things that you didn't do than by the ones you did do. So throw off the bowlines. Sail away from the harbor. Catch the trade winds in your sails. Explore. Dream. Discover."

~Mark Twain

"So many of our dreams at first seem impossible, then they seem improbable, and then, when we summon the will, they soon become inevitable."

~Christopher Reeve

CHAPTER 4

Run Your Own Race

Fear is a natural emotion, one we all struggle with at some point in our lives. Learning to manage our fears can make a significant difference as we pursue our dreams. Many of us have heard that fear is false evidence appearing real. Fear is not real. We become fearful when we take eyes off our goals and what we want; and instead start focusing on what others are saying and doing. The bottom line is that our focus is off. Of course, I experience fear whenever I start something new because of the unknown and unfamiliar. Tony Robbins taught me that when we experience fear it is either because we are afraid of not being loved or not being good enough. Remember, God has not given us a spirit of fear; but of power, love, and a sound mind. We have to learn how to replace our fears with power—to harness those negative notions and replace them with thoughts that inspire, encourage, and empower us. In my experience, managing fear is all about staying focused on what I want and consistently taking action. I have adopted the motto, "DO IT AFRAID" to remind me that I gain power when I take action.

"Most people have no idea of the giant capacity we can immediately command when we focus all of our resources on mastering a single area of our lives." I love this quote from Tony Robbins because it shows the importance of focus. All too often, people are searching for success in all directions. They never take the time to master a single craft in order to discover their true life's passion and purpose. They typically say things like, "I am a jack-of-all-trades!" What they're unaware of is that what they are actually saying translates to, "I am a jack-of-all-trades and master of none!" Although marginal success can be achieved operating in this capacity, we often fall short of the level of success that is truly possible from focused efforts.

Make no mistake about it; what you focus on is what expands. If you focus on what's not working in your life, then more of that will show up for you. However, when you focus on your purpose and what you want for your life, then you will move in that direction with purposeful action and begin to see the results. And I have experienced this truth in my life, time and time again. For example, when I decided to run 26.2 miles, I was one hundred percent focused on that goal. I ran three or four times a week to accomplish that objective. The next year, I decided to run my second marathon. Simply running the race wasn't enough challenge for me. I was determined to better my time. I trained even harder and focused on running even faster.

The first year I ran the marathon with my husband, who at the time was my boyfriend. He was the "veteran" runner, having run for years. I was the novice, so we agreed that we would run the marathon together and keep pace with one another during the race. The next year, for my second marathon, I trained with the goal of bettering my time. He did not have the same goal and did not work towards the same end. During this run, I left him. Because I had trained with a specific focus while he had only maintained his usual routine, I was much better conditioned.

On the course, we bickered back and forth, because he was concerned that I was going too fast and not pacing myself. Initially, he wanted me to slow down to his pace—as he had done the same for me the year before. Finally, he gave me his blessing and sent me off on my own. Much to his surprise, I took off and never looked back. He thought I would burn out and that he would eventually catch up with me. That never happened! I ran full speed to the end, arriving at the finish line a full ten minutes ahead of him. I was focused on improving my time and I did!

My goal here is to help you discover a life that is purposeful, intentional, rewarding, and significant. One of the most important steps on that journey of discovery is staying focused on what you want. You can't get caught up in the goals of others or in what someone else wants for you. Going the distance involves concentrating on running your own race and achieving *your* dreams.

My marathon experience taught me so much about life and what could be accomplished when I focused specifically on a goal. I compare this experience to life's journey towards success because whatever you want for life—that aligns with God's will—can be done with focus and hard work.

Kimberly B. Davis says, "Bring your authentic self to everything you do and success will follow." I remember when I started in the direct sales industry. I thought I needed to mimic my husband and the other female leaders who had all the right traits for this particular business. They looked like success and I wanted to look like that, too. I tried to present information like they did. I copied their actions and moves, hoping to fit in. I didn't trust my own abilities and instead squelched my ideas in favor of their skillful ways. During the time that I tried to imitate others, it should be no surprise that I struggled with my own identity and sense of self. I ultimately failed to connect with prospects and my team because I wasn't being authentic.

The funny thing is, people can sense when you are not being real. I thought I had to wear an extroverted mask to cover up my introverted nature, in order to compete. It wasn't until I became active in a discipleship ministry at church that I realized who I was and what I could offer. Once I discovered who I was and what my unique God-given purpose would be, I was able to shine. And I mean literally shine! People would come up to me and tell me that they saw a light whenever I was around them. I give GOD all of the glory, praise, and honor for that. It is His light shining through me.

I believe that we all have a light and when we live our lives in a way that allows our light to shine its brightest, all of God's riches and glory will fall upon us. We need to stop worrying about others and stop trying to live someone else's life. We are all blessed with our own gifts—we are all equipped to run our own race. We need to live so that our light shines and God gets the glory.

Michael Jordan has said, "Some people want it to happen, some wish it would happen, others make it happen." I have found that the most successful people in the world are the ones who don't just sit around and wait for things to come to them. They go and get it! They are the ones who go the extra mile to make things happen. They don't care what others are doing or rely on anyone else to make their dreams come true. They move into action.

I understood early on that it would be up to me to focus and take action in order to see my dreams manifest into reality. No one else was going to work as hard, commit himself or herself to my dream, or make sacrifices on my behalf in order to achieve the level of success I wanted. Ultimately, these were my goals to accomplish, my dreams to envision. If it was going to be, it was up to me.

Over the years, I have observed people who depend on others to make something happen in their lives. When that person eventually doesn't come through or disappoints them, they get angry and upset. Instead of focusing on their own race—what they need to do—they lose sight and begin to retreat. When you retreat, the life you want just fades in the distance, or gets shoved aside. You find yourself aimlessly drifting, sitting back, waiting and wishing…and nothing happens.

I can recall times when I was aiming to reach a certain level in my company. I could have easily waited for the team to move. I wished for the team to move. I definitely wanted the team to move! The reality was that no one was going to work as hard on my dreams as I would. Instead of sitting around waiting and wishing, I went about making it happen. I stepped up my recruiting efforts. I made extra phone calls to get customer points. I did whatever it took to get to the next level. This was my race and I was determined to run it.

Questions for Reflection

As I have said in this chapter, I believe we all have a light. Take a moment to write down what you think your light might be. This could be any special gift or talents you possess or a unique situation that God has specifically put you in.

I have stressed the importance of remaining authentic and being true to yourself. Make a list of things that you worry about—things that take your focus away from running your own race. How many of these issues are tied to the opinions of others?

I believe that when we tap into our gifts and get real, we can reach people. The list of people that you can reach and influence is different than the list of people I can reach. Take the time to list those in your immediate sphere of influence with whom you can share your light…today.

"Believe in yourself! Have faith in your abilities! Without a humble but reasonable confidence in your own powers you cannot be successful or happy."

~Norman Vincent Peale

"Be miserable. Or motivate yourself. Whatever has to be done, it's always your choice."

~Wayne Dyer

"Learn to get in touch with the silence within yourself, and know that everything in life has purpose. There are no mistakes, no coincidences, all events are blessings given to us to learn from."

~Elisabeth Kubler-Ross

CHAPTER 5

Your Core Group Matters

"You must be the change you want to see in the world." I love this quote from Mahatma Gandhi because I believe in order to bring about positive change in the world we need to engage with our inner world. When you change yourself, from the inside out, you will change your world. If you change how you think, then you will change how you feel and what actions you take. And so the world around you will change. Not only because you are now viewing your environment from a new perspective, but also because the change within can allow you to take action in ways you wouldn't have before.

I believe that you attract to yourself those people and situations that reflect who you are. I can vividly remember during my single days, my girlfriends would tell me that all men were dogs. I listened to their complaints about how all of the good men were taken. They felt that there were no suitable men left for them. I never bought into that type of thinking. I held fast to the belief that as challenging as dating (or developing any kind of relationship) could be, what I put out into the world would be returned to me. When I focused on becoming the best I could be, I was able to find and marry the man of my dreams. I have always seen the reality that Gandhi's idea is true for every aspect of your life. Real change starts with you.

All of us want something in our lives, both from ourselves and from the people around us. We want a more secure financial future. We want better health. We want relationships that fulfill us. We want time and passion to develop our interests. This, and more, is possible. And it all starts with you!

I firmly believe that the energy you put out into the Universe—positive or negative—will come back to you. For that reason, I have always evaluated my relationships through that lens. If I wanted friends who are reliable and trustworthy and reflect the values I aspired to, then I chose friends with those qualities. If a relationship didn't feel good or right, I moved on. I wanted and needed to spend time with people who aligned with my core values and interests. I chose to spend less time with those who brought me down. I realized that I was the sum total of the five people in my circle and that if I wanted to grow to the next level, I was going to get into a new circle. This new circle of friends would help me grow to the next level; they would encourage me, and hold me accountable to my goals. I could learn new strategies, insights, and tools that could take me to the next level. You may find this to be true for yourself. The circle of people that you hang around does matter as you grow to the next level in your life. Choose wisely!

People are in your life for a season, a reason or a lifetime. You may be able to go through your list of friends and find out which category they fall into. Or you may not understand why a friendship didn't last or why a current relationship doesn't feel quite right. When we choose to hang on a little too long to a connection, we may end up limiting our ability to be effective in accomplishing what we desire.

If you want a life that's different than the life you currently have, you can't expect it to happen without doing anything to cause it. You need to step up to the plate with your own actions and personal changes. Without that, you can't really expect other people or other aspects of your life to change merely because that's what you want.

Look around at the elements of your life that you're unhappy with. In almost every case, there are steps you can take to make things better. Be the change you want to see in your world. If you want something different, it's up to you to get the ball rolling with actions, not with mere words.

I believe that one person can make a difference in the world. This takes effort and requires a high level of self-awareness, a belief in yourself, and a strong commitment. You must be confident in what you believe and bold enough to live an authentic life. When I look out at the ordinary people who do extraordinary things every day, I am reminded that we all have the power to impact the world—one person at a time.

A friend of mine, Quenesha McNair, is one of those ordinary people who make a difference in the world. Her courage and commitment to youth inspire me. When she was growing up in rural North Carolina, Quenesha's love of experiencing new things and finding inspiration in the world around her served her well as she got involved in many opportunities to expand her horizons. In 2007, she created a foundation called beGlobal. This non-profit organization encourages young people from rural areas by giving them the opportunity to work with international peers in their communities. She developed the beGlobal program so that youth could learn more about the world around them and give back to their communities.

When I began my own foundation in 2011, I looked to Quenesha's example and knew I wanted to be a part of impacting our youth. I had the vision of exposing pre-teens and young adults to a world that they hadn't before been exposed to. I wanted to show them a world of possibility, where the only limits were self-imposed.

In Proverbs 27:17, it is written, "As iron sharpens iron, so one man sharpens another." In this simple statement lies a big impact—your core group matters. God grows us through many different methods. It may be through spending time in His Word or maybe a trial or test we endure. One method He uses to produce growth is fellowship through our relationships.

Our edge can be restored, our iron sharpened, through strong friendships within the body of Christ. By learning from and teaching each other, we hone our gifts. We need the feedback, encouragement, and counsel of others. But it is important to note that the verse says, "Iron sharpens iron." In other words, iron must come into contact with iron in order to be sharpened. This means that we can't be sharpened by just any individual—we can only be sharpened by certain individuals. If you want to be sharpened mentally, you must interact with mentally sharp individuals. If you want to be sharpened spiritually, you must interact with spiritually mature individuals. If you want to be sharpened morally, you must interact with morally pure and upright individuals.

Paul spoke of the importance of coming into contact with the right people in I Corinthians 15:33, "Do not be deceived: 'Bad company corrupts good morals.' " Paul is talking about those people with whom we associate or have fellowship. We tend to take on the character of the group with which we associate. If we associate with people of bad character, they will succeed in pulling us down to their level.

It is not likely that we will succeed in pulling them up. It is much easier to go down than to go up, especially if those with whom you keep company have no reason to go up, being comfortable with the level at which they are at the time.

Surrounding myself with friends such as Quenesha gives me hope and inspiration that I too can make a difference in this world. I believe when you can positively impact a young person, you can also have an impact on a family. When you impact a family, you further impact a neighborhood. When you impact a neighborhood, you can impact a city. By impacting a city, you go on to influence a state. Influencing a state affects a nation, which then goes on to impact the world. In this manner, we can change the world, one person at a time!

Questions for Reflection

God blesses us so that we can bless others. Think of some of the things you can give back to the world, through the specific gifts God has given you. Take the time to write them down.

As we looked at the verse in Proverbs about an iron sharpening an iron, we see how important it is to surround ourselves with positive influences. Write down some of the people in your life who have had a big impact on your life. Be sure to include the reasons why these people have been influential to you.

Now that you've made a list of people who have been a positive influence in your life, take the time to write down the names of those *you* want to encourage. This could be a specific individual, or it could be a group such as young people or the elderly.

"Some come and leave, fulfilling a single purpose; others, for a time or a season to teach us by sharing their experiences; and last, a select few who participate forever with relationships that endure through eternity."

~Jaren L. Davis

"Surround yourself with only people who are going to lift you higher."

~Oprah Winfrey

"Align yourself with people that you can learn from, people who want more out of life, people who are stretching and searching and seeking some higher ground in life."

~Les Brown

CHAPTER 6

Get to the Root

"You were born to win, but to be the winner you were born to be, you must plan to win and prepare to win. Then, and only then, can you legitimately expect to win." This quote from Zig Ziglar was a great source of motivation for me. It helped me to understand that we are all born with a spirit of power and self-discipline. It helped me to find the winner within me and in fact, it should be an encouragement that we are all, in fact, born to win! There is a winner in you—I know this and it is important that you believe this for yourself. But tapping into the winner within is only part of the process. You must also plan to win and prepare to win. You might be asking yourself, what does that look like?

Oprah has been quoted as saying, "Real courage is the courage not to give up on your dreams." In essence, this is getting to the root of winning—having the courage to plan and prepare to win even before you take the first step forward.

The reality is that most women may never realize their full potential because they don't first believe that they are winners. Many are successful on the outside, but on the inside, feel trapped and empty. Why is that?

Well for me, I can say it was because of the baggage I carried from my childhood, a failed marriage, setbacks in my career, and countless financial mistakes. I wasn't sure whether I was afraid of success or didn't think I was worthy of it. I believe it was a little bit of both. Although I was successful in my corporate career, I still felt unfulfilled. I felt there was more in me and that there was more for me to do. You can probably identify with my feelings.

After I started my business, I realized that I had to get to the root of what was holding me back if I was going to win in my business and in my life. I began to reflect on my life. What I learned about myself was that I was creating stories about my life. The truth was none of the stories that I told myself were real. They were all made up based on my view of the way my world should be. I created a story that I had to dress a certain way, have a certain level of education, and speak a certain way to be considered a success. This was a lie because I define my success, not society. I created the story that if I didn't spend every waking hour of every day with my kids and was the soccer mom, it meant I wasn't a good mother. This was a lie because my love for my kids is not measured in the quantity of time I spend with them but instead in the quality of time I spend with them. I created the story that because I failed at marriage at a young age that it meant I was a failure. This was a lie because I am not a failure but had made a bad decision that I was able to learn and grow from. I created the story that if someone disagreed with me, then it meant I am not smart. This was a lie because not everyone is going to agree with me all the time, and as long as I am true to myself, they don't have to.

What I learned is that some of my childhood experiences shaped these beliefs. I am the oldest of five sisters. Growing up, I set high standards for myself because I felt I had to be a good example at all times for my younger siblings. I had imposed unrealistic expectations on myself and set the bar way too high. Many women are guilty of setting high, and sometimes unrealistic, expectations for themselves that can become the source of many frustrations and limitations. For a long time, I lived as though failure was simply not an option. I felt pressure to be the best at everything. I was afraid to stumble for fear of disappointing my mom and family. Living in this story caused me to not only doubt my abilities and myself, but to sabotage my success because I believed that if I didn't have all of the "right" information, I couldn't move forward; although successful people fail many times on their journey. This was not an authentic way to live and it did not feel good.

All the stories were lies that I—no one else—made up, and as long as I chose to live in the story, then I would not and could not win. When I realize that I am stuck in my story, I remind myself that nothing has meaning except the meaning that I give it. I then shift my focus to what I want and where I am going, and I gain power to move past the situation.

Think about all the situations and circumstances you have overcome to get where you are today. Most of us have dealt with, and prevailed over, some major obstacles just to be where we are. I want to challenge you to get rid of any negative, disempowering stories you have been telling yourself. See the positive side of everything you have gone through and attach a positive and empowering story. When you do that, your focus then shifts from what went wrong to what can I learn to help me grow more into the person that I am! Always remember, your test is your testimony that can bless someone.

Angela Thomas says, "God changes our focus so we can see His power in our weakness." In life, as we go through the inevitable ups and downs, we often focus on figuring out "why" something has happened. This can be a distraction that keeps us from moving past difficult circumstances. We are all faced with challenges. However, if we change our perspective and see these challenges as opportunities to learn and to grow, things begin to change for us. One thing that has helped me focus through the down times is to listen for God speaking to me. Once I began to view obstacles as a way for God to get my attention—I gave it to Him and He showed me who I really am! I became less stressed about the problem and more open to learn the lesson so I could grow to the next level.

I adopted the mindset that I could overcome, that God would not put more on me than I could handle.

"No temptation has seized you except what is common to man. And God is faithful; He will not let you be tempted beyond what you can bear. But when you are tempted, He will also provide a way out so that you can stand up under it." 1 Corinthians 10:13

This verse became my personal battle cry when I set out to win. I clung to the expectation of winning, despite any obstacle in my way. I believed that God would not give me more than I could handle. And no matter what situation I found myself in, I knew I had what I needed to deal with it sufficiently. I found it reassuring to know that any temptation that has overtaken me (including the story that I wasn't good enough for the goals I had set) is common to all people. Instead of excusing my particular situation as unique or special, it gave me strength to know that other women of God have faced similar temptations and found the strength, through God, to overcome. I know I can be victorious in the strength of Jesus!

So, like an overprotective parent who won't let her children wander aimlessly through the candy store because they don't have the ability to resist temptation, God keeps us from things we cannot handle. Of course, what we can and cannot handle changes from moment to moment.

God has promised not only to limit our temptation, but also to provide a way of escape in tempting times. He will never force us to use the way of escape, but He will make the way of escape. It's up to us to take God's way of escape.

Whatever I am going through, I know it is for a reason. I know that I need to take personal responsibility and figure out the lesson to be learned from each "storm." No matter what I go through, I do not view myself as a victim to circumstance, but rather a victor.

Knowing that God will shield you from situations that you cannot handle, and realizing that He will give you the strength to deal with any obstacle set in your path, you can move forward and claim victory. To get back to the quote from Zig Ziglar, you can accept that you were born to win so know that you can plan to win, prepare to win, and expect to win!

How do you plan to win? You begin by creating a clear vision for your life.

Habakkuk 2:2 says, *"Write down the vision so that you can read it and run with it."*

When you can see it, it becomes real. Write your vision out clearly so you know exactly where you are going. Then put it where you can see it every day. I put mine on my bathroom mirror.

Then make an action plan, mapping out the steps needed to put your vision into effect. You will want to review your vision regularly, in order to understand the value and purpose of your aspiration. This helps you stay focused on your ultimate goal and gives you motivation to continue even during the difficult times. Make your vision be your motivation.

How do you prepare to win? Now that you have laid the foundation and have a clear vision to follow, look around for the possibilities to bring your concept to life. See the opportunities that exist—they may be all around you, or you may need to create favorable conditions. I encourage you to seek wise counsel at this critical time and be sure to surround yourself with positive influences—people who will support your vision.

You will have to set short- and long-term goals. You want evaluate, adjust, and possibly strengthen your goals along the way.

To help you overcome your next goal stumbling block, here is what I did.

Defined my goals. Goals can be modified, changed, adapted, and shaped as you progress.

Developed my plan. A goal always needs a plan—once you have your goals, devise a plan to go with each goal. A plan is a step-by-step blueprint of how to get from where you are now, to where you need to be to achieve that goal.

Began with the end in mind. Start with the big picture and get smaller—set your big mega-goals, work your way back and set micro-goals that lead up to your ultimate goal. If you can achieve all of your micro-goals with ease, then getting your mega-goals right will be easy.

Set my priorities. Where do your priorities lie—is it with education, career, finance, family, health, pleasure, attitude, creativity, or public service? Decide where God wants you to be and try to invest as much time as you can there, without sacrificing any other essential parts of your life.

Used the SMART goal initiative. SMART stands for S: Specific, M: Measurable, A: Attainable, R: Relevant, T: Time sensitive. If your goals can meet all of these criteria, you're on your way to a good plan.

Wrote down my goals. Put your goals in words, and place them somewhere visible. Read them often; think about them even more. Performance goals will take you places, but you have to be working towards them constantly to make them count.

Was realistic about what I could do by when. Be as realistic as you can—keep your goals realistic or scale them to the point where they make sense but will still stretch you.

Focus is what you're aiming for. If you don't want your goals enough to focus on them all day, every day—then maybe they need to be reassessed.

How do you expect to win? You adopt the mindset that you can overcome obstacles that will come your way, and that you will be successful as long as you stay the course. You approach each day with the expectation of winning. When you expect to win, you can encourage and motivate yourself to get to the finish line. You can also inspire and raise others along the way.

NAACP Image Award-nominated author BeNeca Ward has gained much notice for her outstanding literary work in the book *3rd Generation Country.* In it, she writes these inspiring words about the importance of recognizing the winner that is inside each one of us.

"My mother sat me down and said, ...you are beautiful to me but you must know that you are beautiful for yourself. You should also be aware that true beauty is in the eye of the beholder, which means that how beautiful you are to other people is always going to be subjective to who is looking at you at that time, and since you will always be looking at yourself first, you should find your own beauty and feel good about who you are. She went on to tell me that I needed to take the time to identify those things that I found to be beautiful about myself but also celebrate what I thought was weird or unusual because those were the special things that God had given to me that made me different from everybody else. I learned how to appreciate, embrace, and enhance those special things so that they would shine rather than be hidden...We learned to love and identify with what made us uniquely beautiful."

Get to the root of who you are—a woman filled with purpose and a winner. With God's steady guidance, a firm belief in yourself, and a clear purpose to fulfill, you will always be a victor in this life.

Questions for Reflection

We discussed the importance of replacing negative stories with positive stories that empower you. Identify any story you have told yourself that you realize now is holding you back from being all that you are.

Make a list of obstacles you have overcome to get where you are today. Include any challenges, big or small, that you see as something you have overcome in life.

When you look back at your challenges and obstacles, can you see the opportunities you've had to learn? What are some ways in which God has spoken to you?

With a renewed vision of yourself as a winner, who expects to win, write down your aspirations and what you want to accomplish.

"God will not permit any troubles to come upon us, unless He has a specific plan by which great blessing can come out of the difficulty."

~Peter Marshall

"Our goals can only be reached through a vehicle of a plan, in which we must fervently believe, and upon which we must vigorously act. There is no other route to success."

~Pablo Picasso

"Choose your friends with caution; plan your future with purpose, and frame your life with faith."

~Thomas S. Monson

CHAPTER 7

Show Up Every Day

The training program I used when preparing for my first marathon called for me to run several days a week, as well as EVERY Saturday morning at 6 a.m. Do you think there were times when I didn't feel like getting up at 5 a.m. to run on a Saturday morning? ABSOLUTELY! But I did, and no matter how I felt, I made the effort to show up every time.

In your life, you will find you have to show up every day to work harder on yourself than you do on your own job. Les Brown is quoted as saying, "When you stop fighting for what you want, what you don't want will show up." Going after the life you are dreaming of will not always be easy. It's going to require a healthy dose of dedication, discipline, and determination. Know that when you've reached your goals, all that you have gone through will have been worth it. It's not just about the destination, but the journey along the way to making your dreams a reality. The journey allows you to learn more about yourself, what you are capable of, and how much power you really have. My journey has revealed so much to me about me. It has revealed the good, the bad, and the ugly. I improved on the good to get to the great, refined the bad, and eradicated the ugly. I continue to grow and develop because I realize that no matter how far I grow, there is always another level of success. I have to show up and do the good to great work on me daily. I want to encourage you to show up every day, embrace who you are becoming along the way, and do the good to great work on yourself.

"It's not what's happening to you now or what has happened in your past that determines who you become. Rather, it's your decisions about what to focus on, what things mean to you, and what you're going to do about them that will determine your ultimate destiny." This quote from Tony Robbins sums up the power behind making decisions and following through on them.

More than anything else, your decisions determine your future. The decisions that you make set you apart from the rest. They determine if you live the life you love, or don't. Moment to moment, we are faced with a decision to make. For example, you may begin with the determination to put all of your efforts towards pursuing your dreams. This leads you to make decisions on what steps you must take in order to make your dreams a reality. These choices may include expanding your knowledge, networking, and making the right connections, or starting your own business. Every decision—big and small—you make matters. If you decide to just sit around and make excuses, you will reap the consequences of those decisions. Your life is a result of the decisions that you've made. The truth is that the key to changing yourself comes down to a simple concept: making a decision. Once you decide who you want to be, you must take action and start the journey to becoming that person. This journey of transformation is fulfilling because you will learn so much about yourself. Be careful not to compare yourself to others along the way. This is a tragic mistake that most people make because the reality is that we are all unique. And so your journey is going to be different.

Life is constantly evolving and the same thinking or action that got you where you are right now will need to evolve and grow in order to get you to the next level, whatever that looks like for you. Your best thinking has gotten you to where you are right now. If you don't show up every day—life will pass you by.

Growing up, I was the quiet, shy introvert. I was usually the last one to speak up in class and was always afraid of speaking in public. I found success in other ways—I was smart academically and I worked hard to achieve success in Corporate America. And yet, I was always afraid. The day I began a business in the direct sales industry, I was way out of my comfort zone!

It took six months before I fully understood the power of the direct sales industry. After reading success stories of people who got their start in a similar way, I learned that anyone with a desire for change and the determination to win can be successful in this industry. I could make my dreams a reality! However, I had a big obstacle in my way—I would have to overcome my fear of public speaking.

Bill Cosby said, "Decide that you want it more than you are afraid of it." I already knew I was afraid of public speaking, but for the first time in my life I wanted something and acquiring that something would mean I would have to decide to get past the hurdle of speaking up in front of a crowd. Just like training for a marathon, I had to show up every day and face my fears. Once I did, I began to feel empowered and encouraged. I can't say that my fears completely went away; in fact, I often failed forward. I learned from my mistakes and kept advancing. To take advantage of the many opportunities, I had to practice, practice, practice—I went from bad to good to great. Over time, I gained the confidence to move past my fears and to go straight to the top.

In four short years, I was able to walk away from my full-time, six-figure salaried job and rise to the top of the compensation plan in my company. This was with no real prior experience in the industry, but a strong commitment to put myself out there every day and the determination to see it through.

In Galatians 6:9 it states, "And let us not grow weary of doing good, for in due season we will reap, if we do not give up." When a farmer sows a crop, he doesn't just reap the seeds he has planted; he gathers plants that will allow him to grow even more crops. As we wisely manage our resources before God under the principle of sowing and reaping, we need patience. This is because the harvest does not come immediately after you sow the seeds. We must not give up during the lull between the hard work of sowing and the reward of reaping. When the work is hard and painful, the waiting can make us feel like our efforts are unrewarded. It's easy to lose heart when we feel like that, but that is exactly when we must hang on and not grow weary. Your work is still in progress, so stay focused and positive, all the while moving forward.

"There is a sowing season and a reaping season and they are not the same season." This quote from Bob Proctor illustrates that true success and fulfillment takes time. You have to put in a lot of hard work and make many sacrifices before you may begin to see the fruits of your labor. I refer to the period of time when we are investing our time, energy, and talents into a process before we can see the results, as "sowing seeds." Some of the seeds I planted along my journey included putting myself out there and making an effort to meet new people. I read books and studied the industry—I was and still am curious to learn the secrets behind others' success. I continued to invest in my own personal growth and development. The compound effect states that simple, small, and consistent steps taken over time will create success. It did for me and it can for you!

In today's world, it's all about instant gratification. Everywhere you turn, you see a culture of people deeply entrenched in the desire to get what they want, when they want it—the concept of waiting has become almost foreign to younger generations. Most people have very little patience, which can lead to adopting a mindset that if something is meant to happen, it will happen quickly. If success isn't achieved immediately, people become discouraged and give up. The reality in most cases is that not enough seeds may have been sown, or the seeds have not matured enough to be harvested. True success rarely happens overnight. While you wait for your seeds to blossom, enjoy the journey that is uniquely yours. Embrace what you learn along the way, continue to show up every day to cultivate your crop, and eventually you will see amazing results.

For me, this is a lot like gaining or losing weight. There have been periods in my life when I have eaten like crazy—consuming all of my favorite foods, regardless of whether they were good for me or not. The first few days of overeating were fun, I won't kid you! I began to think, "This is great! I haven't gained a single pound." Over time, of course, I would begin to see the results of my eating. I'm sure you may have been there—one day you're feeling good, the next day the weight suddenly shows up. I was reaping the harvest, literally!

When I set out to lose weight, I would work out and diet for weeks before I would ever see the slightest dent in the scale. Naturally, I would begin to feel very frustrated because I wanted immediate results. We all do, right? I had to remind myself that I wouldn't see the consequences of my hard effort right away. But that didn't mean I should just give up. I ultimately stayed focused on losing weight, on "sowing my seeds" through continued exercise and eating healthier foods. Over time, the positive choices I made and consistently worked toward paid off and I was able to reap the benefits of a healthy lifestyle. This is a very simple example of how the compound effect works.

Questions for Reflection

Can you name one (or more) decisions you have made in the past that have had a major impact on your life? Take the time to list any decisions that have served as a turning point for you.

I decided to overcome something that caused me anxiety because my desire to succeed was more powerful than my fear of speaking in public. Make a list of obstacles or challenges that are currently holding you back from reaching your full potential.

Can you think of some areas in your life where you have reaped what you have sown? Are there times when you have sown and are still waiting for the harvest to come in? It may be that the results you are looking for are just around the corner—so keep at it!

"Believe in yourself. You gain strength, courage, and confidence by every experience in which you stop to look fear in the face...You must do that which you think you cannot do."

~Eleanor Roosevelt

"Eighty percent of success is showing up."

~Woody Allen

"Nothing in the world can take the place of Persistence. Talent will not; nothing is more common than unsuccessful men with talent. Genius will not; unrewarded genius is almost a proverb. Education will not; the world is full of educated derelicts. Persistence and determination alone are omnipotent. The slogan 'Press On' has solved and always will solve the problems of the human race."

~Calvin Coolidge

CHAPTER 8

Push Yourself

The night before I was set to run ten miles—in a row!—for the first time, I spent some time reflecting on how I had gotten to this point. I had certainly pushed myself through a great deal of physical pain. I had battled the constant feeling of wanting to just give up. My mind kept returning to my initial self-defeating thoughts. I had a great deal of doubt and disbelief that I struggled with. I was so convinced that I wasn't a runner, let alone a long-distance competitor, that I devoted a lot of time and energy into talking myself out of training for a marathon. The same was the case when I started my business. I struggled in the very beginning because I just didn't believe I could be successful. I didn't believe in me.

Thankfully, I am not a quitter. I don't believe you are either. But, if we are not careful, our self-limiting beliefs can deter us from becoming who we are and getting to where we are going. I knew that I had to transform my negative self-talk into positive affirmations if I was ever going to see this through. I began to say to myself, "Just take it one step at a time because life is about the steps you take to get to the end." One step at a time eventually turned into one mile at a time. My new affirmation and determination to push myself through the challenges ahead prepared me not only to complete the physical race; they inspired me to win the marathon of my life. To me, winning the marathon of my life started with finding my unique purpose in life. From that point on, I was able to push myself through my doubts and self-imposed limitations to find the courage to persevere.

Going after your dreams is about pushing yourself harder than anyone else will. During the training days and especially on race day, I realized that I could only rely on myself to complete the task. The same is true for pursuing your dreams. As Oprah Winfrey says, "You are responsible for your own life." At the end of each day, you alone face yourself in the mirror and account for the actions you did (or didn't) take in pursuit of your goals and dreams. You alone will have to create an environment for yourself that positions you for peak performance. While it's important to surround yourself with people who inspire and motivate you to your personal best, it is up to you to transform that motivation into action. Once you accept this, you can have consistent forward progress in every area of your life.

There is a famous quote from Siddhartha that states, "There are two mistakes one can make along the road to truth…not going all the way and not starting." Over and over again, I see people who embark on starting their business. Their energy and enthusiasm are contagious! They are eager to learn all they can and talk about how determined they are to get to the top. These people have a strong compelling "why" for building their business and they seem to have all the right words and make all the right moves. I am always ready to help them, to come alongside and guide them towards success. However, time and time again, as soon as adversity hits, it's all over. They quit.

To be quite honest, it is really disappointing to witness these failures. In the beginning of my career, I often took these letdowns personally. I was amazed that someone who had been so excited and eager, ready to go the distance to make his or her dreams come true, could be so easily dissuaded. How did that happen? I was prepared to help them do all they could, but I soon realized that I couldn't help them if they didn't want it badly enough for themselves to push through. It was a tragedy to watch people give up on themselves and their bright futures, but ultimately, there was little I could do.

When I think of my own journey to the top of my company's compensation plan, I look back at the drive I had to develop in order to push myself past so many obstacles. I had to push myself beyond my comfort zone, leap over my fears, and shove past my self-imposed limitations. I had to work harder on transforming myself than I had to work on the job itself! It took me a year and a half before I came to the realization that I had everything I needed to succeed. It was within me the whole time. God had equipped me with everything I needed in order to fulfill His purpose for my life.

Isaiah 40:28-31 reads, "Do you not know? Have you not heard? The LORD is the everlasting God, the Creator of the ends of the earth. He will not grow tired or weary, and His understanding no one can fathom. He gives strength to the weary and increases the power of the weak. Even youths grow tired and weary, and young men stumble and fall; but those who hope in the Lord will renew their strength. They will soar on wings like eagles; they will run and not grow weary, they will walk and not be faint." How easily we convince ourselves that while God has infinite power, He is unable to meet our particular, personal needs. Isaiah explains that one benefit we can receive from God is that He gives us His great power.

How do we receive this strength from the Lord? We wait on Him. This is not a passive, sitting around kind of waiting. This is not hitting the snooze button until God makes a move. He brings strength to us as we seek Him and rely on Him, when we depend on Him, rather than on our own strength. What kind of strength does He equip us with? "They shall mount up on wings like eagles." He gives us the strength to soar above everything else. In life, we are often limited by our own doubts and fears. For every little voice in our head that says we can't succeed, there may be the real voice of a friend or loved one who echoes the same negative thoughts. The reason He gives us this power is so that we can move forward, in His purpose. We can rise above the voices of naysayers. When the hardness of life exhausts us, and we find ourselves weary, God is here to give us strength. If only we will wait on Him!

The legendary golfer Ben Hogan is quoted as saying, "The more I practice, the luckier I get." This quote sums up the reason why I continued to run, even on my "off" days. It's why I committed to building my business until I reached the top. Despite any adversity, obstacle, or struggle I faced, I kept on practicing. Hard work and perseverance do pay off with the fruits of reaching your goals, finding success, and creating new opportunities for you and your future.

I love to surround myself with people who appreciate the efforts of hard work and who inspire me with their own pursuits. My nail technician, Kathy, is one of the hardest working individuals I know. She owns and manages a couple of nail salons, often putting in long hours every day working with clients. In addition, she takes college courses and is a single mother raising three children who range in age from five to seventeen.

One day, I asked her why she pushes herself so much. She explained to me that she worked hard because she had no other option. While she had been married, she and her husband were living the American dream—they had it all. Unfortunately, on August 23, 2005, Hurricane Katrina struck and they lost everything. The impact of the disaster, coupled with the fact that her husband lost work because of the storm, left them devastated. Even after the physical effects of the storm had worn off, their marriage suffered a personal storm, and as a result, Kathy and her husband divorced. I am sure that she felt like giving up many times. I see how hard she works and find so much inspiration from her example of perseverance and determination to make a better life for her children and herself. I have learned that it takes all that, and more, to reach where you are trying to go.

Questions for Reflection

We've seen that good things come to those who wait, but only those things that are left by those who hustle! What achievement or aspiration are you waiting to begin working towards? Make a list and note the reason why you are waiting.

What can you do to push yourself towards that next step in achieving your goal? If possible, write down some logical steps that you can take that will help you progress to the next level (these can be baby steps!).

Luck is when hard work meets opportunity. Take a moment to think of some areas where you have been working diligently but not seeing any fruit. Make a list of these areas and ask yourself if you are doing everything you can to get the results you want to have.

“Inaction breeds doubt and fear. Action breeds confidence and courage. If you want to conquer fear, do not sit home and think about it. Go out and get busy.”

~Dale Carnegie

“If we don’t change, we don’t grow. If we don’t grow, we aren’t really living.”

~Gail Shelly

“For true success ask yourself four questions: Why? Why not? Why not me? Why not now?”

~James Allen

CHAPTER 9

Purposeful Action

Tyler Perry, now a household name known for his movies and plays, wasn't always a writer, producer, and director. It was a simple piece of advice that he heard one day while watching the Oprah Winfrey show that changed his life forever. Encouraged to write down his thoughts and experiences, Perry realized that he had stories he wanted to share, ideas he wanted to impart to others. He began writing a series of letters to himself, in the voice of different characters. These letters eventually became the basis for a musical, *I Know I've Been Changed*. Perry weathered many cycles of working, saving money, and putting on his play before he finally found success.

Perry offers advice to those who are seeking to become who they really are, and for those who want to put their vision into action. Plant the seed of who you want to be and water that seed, believe in it. Many factors may contribute to its growth, but you have to believe in the decision, in order to give it roots. Perry says that we all get scattered in different directions, following every shifting idea that comes into our head. But what separates the doers from the dreamers is that the doers make choices and stick with it until they make it a reality.

When you find yourself struggling with a decision about how to make a change in your life, there are certain motions you might go through. You could create a lengthy list of pros and cons, seek wise counsel from friends, or pray and search for spiritual insight.

In the end, despite all of the input and well-meaning intentions, it is up to you to make a choice.

Life is not easy. We have all dealt with disappointments and setbacks. These can range from failed relationships to the loss of a job, or a wayward child. Of course, this is only a short list of what we have to deal with as we go through life. The reality is, if you live long enough, the rain will come. Storms will enter our lives only to leave, with destruction in their wake. When that happens, all we can do is make a decision on how we want to deal with that particular storm. We can choose to lie down and surrender, accepting circumstances as they are, or we can get up, fight, and find our way through the downpour. In other words, we can make the choice to change the way things are—YES, you have that power—we all do! And then you have to act on that choice. You have to continue to take action by moving purposefully in the direction of your dream.

The most important thing to understand about storms is that they won't last forever. Even when it seems like a never-ending barrage of difficult circumstances, eventually the sun will shine again. The key to survival and success is that despite the storm, you must have faith and keep up the good fight. Without the elements of determination and faith, you will end up settling in life. You will continue to get all of the things that you say you don't want. Is it hard to fight? Of course! Will you want to give up? Yes! But you must not, because the simple truth is that as long as God has blessed you with another day, you must get up, go out and fight. There are people out there who need to be blessed by the testimony only you can share.

My brother-in-law, Tim Richards, is a shining example of the importance of making choices and taking purposeful actions that allow blessings to be shared to empower others. What I have learned is that when you live to empower and serve others, God gives you power to do more!

In December 2005, Tim was diagnosed with pancreatic cancer and given only months to live. Almost seven years later, he is still here—and he is thriving and literally "fighting like hell." Tim serves as an inspiration to so many people and is a wonderful testimony of God's miraculous power. Every day he experiences pain, but to see him you would never know that. His warm smile and encouraging words are a motivation not only for our immediate family, but also for all of those people who come in contact with Tim on a regular basis.

Tim has endured thirty-two major surgeries, some of which have taken him to the brink of death. However, due to God's grace and mercy, combined with Tim's sheer will to fight for life, he is still here. Tim has shared how some days are better than others, but even on the roughest days, he does not surrender to defeat. He works out regularly in the gym, travels, and dedicates his time to pursuing interests and people who bring meaning and purpose to his life.

Tim's journey is an example of how we all need to live our lives and fight for our dreams. We can easily give into our feelings and circumstances, but at the end of the day, the best choice is to fight for what we want, so that we too can lead a life that is full of meaning and purpose. Tim made his choice in 2005 to not just survive, but to thrive, and continues to take purposeful action with each day he is given.

Isaiah 30:21 states, "Whether you turn to the right or to the left, your ears will hear a voice behind you, saying, 'This is the way; walk in it.' " This is one of the promises found in His word, where God promises to guide and navigate our steps. This verse assures us that when we come to making decisions and taking action, the Lord will tell us which way to go. The Holy Spirit lives in us, and we have the promise that God will guide us whether to "turn left or turn right" when it comes to our next steps! We may not literally hear the voice of the Lord speaking behind us, but we can be sure that God will not leave us alone when it comes to the decisions we must make in life.

Oprah Winfrey is quoted as saying, "Doing the best at this moment puts you in the best place for the next moment." I have learned that everything that happens in my life happens for a reason, and each situation serves me in some way. As such, I seek to learn the lesson. Have you ever had an extremely difficult situation occur in your life? Not just an inconvenience or something that made you uncomfortable—I'm talking about a situation that brings you to your knees. If you have, my best comfort is to remind you that there is always a lesson to be learned from everything that happens in our lives. Even in the most difficult moments, there is a reason and a lesson to be imparted. It is my belief that when we learn the lesson intended for us, we can move forward, better prepared for the next adventure God has in store for us. You can choose to be a victim or you can choose to be a victor in the circumstances that surround you. The choice is yours.

Questions for Reflection

Make a list of circumstances in your life that have been especially challenging. Beside each situation, write whether you view yourself as a victim or a victor in each particular instance. It is my hope that this exercise will allow you to see that you have a choice in how you view your circumstances. You may someday revisit this entry with an entirely new perspective.

Take time to reflect on the life you have chosen to this point. What changes would you like to see?

Make a list of changes that feel especially challenging at the moment. Think of the changes you could make that will help expand the vision you have for yourself and your future.

"Both heroes and victims face setbacks. The distinction between those two groups is that heroes stand up, while victims give up."

~Jon Gordon

"Life is change. Growth is optional. Choose wisely."

~Unknown

"Life is 10% what happens to you and 90% how you respond to it."

~Lou Holtz

BONUS

Why, as women, do we not challenge ourselves, and push to reach our greatest potential? There is so much this world has to offer you, if you only take the time to discover God's plan for your life. Hopefully, now that you've read *Faith, Focus, Action*—you know where to start.

Just remember these three little rules and you too can have a purpose-driven life.

Start where you are, right now! Don't let your past define your future.

Make sure that you show up every day, it's really half the battle.

Push yourself. There is always more!

God has equipped you to be the kind of woman who can make it, because of your wonderful and fulfilling talents. So, take that step forward—even if it scares you. Put all of your faith in God that things will turn out better than okay for you.

Don't forget to believe in yourself as well. Without a strong, confident self-image—getting things right will be an uphill battle.

Have the faith to focus on the things in your life that will make you better at what you do. Hone in on them, perfect them, and don't let go until you are making incredible things happen in your niche. God has made you perfect, and you can do these awesome things!

Finally, when things get tough—that's when you need to push through and draw nearer to God. Everything happens for a reason. Taking action will change your life. Good or bad, your decisions will affect who you are now, and who you will become. It's all in your hands.

So be great. Do outstanding things. Be on fire for God while following His life plan for you. And one day you'll wake up and realize that you've made it. God wants you to—and if you listen carefully enough, you'll understand why.

Conclusion

One morning more than forty years ago, an amazing message was played for a group of salespeople at Earl Nightingale's insurance agency. The sales force was instantly energized by what they heard, and quickly acted. The message began to spread and soon requests came in for copies of the recording.

Within no time, thousands of people had called, written, or walked into Earl's office to ask about the message. Today, that number is well into the millions and *The Strangest Secret* remains one of the most motivational messages ever recorded. I know it transformed my life when I heard it. One aspect in particular stood out for me. On the recording, Earl mentions that one of the problems with people achieving success is that most people conform. I thought about what that meant—when we conform to what the masses are doing, the result can be that we fail to achieve any real success on our own. We don't fulfill our unique purpose.

One day, in 2002, I got the opportunity of a lifetime, a chance to step off the path I had been on, step out into the purpose God intended for my life and become who I am today. The opportunity came in the form of a setback—a job loss. I will never forget the day my boss flew in from Atlanta, called me into a conference room with Human Resources on the line, and proceeded to inform me that this would be my last day with the company.

To say I was shocked and amazed at this situation would be an understatement! A sense of sadness and failure swept over me as I listened to the details unfold. I worried about how I would tell people and what they would think of me.

What I understand now, that I didn't at the time, was that everything happens for a reason and it serves us. That was a day that my life changed. It wasn't a decision that I would have made for myself but it made me realize that one decision can have a profound effect on your life forever. The only aspect of this particular decision I could control was how I reacted to it. Charles R. Swindoll says life is ten percent what happens to you and ninety percent how you react to it.

Sometimes we need to be pushed so that we can reach our destiny, our true calling! Truth be told, I had gotten complacent with a job and a paycheck, and all the stuff that comes along with it. I am sure you can relate—you want all the stuff, you go after all the stuff, and you get all the stuff. But you eventually find that the pursuit leaves you without either the time or money (or both) to enjoy the stuff. You are now caught up in the rat race, working hard but not working smart. As a result, you forget about the big dreams and the plans you once had for your life. Life becomes empty and meaningless, void of purpose and fulfillment.

The decision that resulted in me losing my job ultimately changed my mindset and was the motivation that I needed to go after my heart's desire and pursue something of my own. I began to consider starting my own business and so I began to look for the right business opportunity for me. I found it in 5LINX. Oftentimes when life puts us in undesirable circumstances, we begin to shift our thinking. We realize that there is more to life than we had been taught up to that moment. And then we begin the journey of self-discovery to get to the life that is full of purpose and meaning. It's the time when we start the journey to becoming. It all begins with a thought that propels us into focus and action. When we change our thoughts, we can change our lives.

Abraham Lincoln said, "Things may come to those who wait, but only the things left by those who hustle."

You can't stroll leisurely towards a goal, you've got to hustle; you must move quickly in order to gain the momentum necessary to escape the gravitational pull of the mundane. The best things in life come to those who hustle. Are you hustling? Many of us crave success in this life. We yearn to achieve our goals and live out our wildest dreams. We want it bad! However, few are willing to step out beyond their comfort zone in order to achieve the triumph they long for. Many are waiting on something to happen, or someone else to take action, in order for them to move forward. This is a dangerous place to be in because the truth is, no one else is going to move for you. You have to get up and go out every day and hustle.

Do you know that while you are waiting, hoping that something will take off, there is a group of people who understand the core of Lincoln's message? They have taken it to heart and are hustling right now for what they want. They are moving and taking action towards achieving their dreams.

In the end, Abraham Lincoln didn't live to become an old man. However, in the years he was alive, he made a profound impact on the world. Are you making your years count? Are you changing the world? You're capable of it; if you're able to read and understand these words, then you have the ability to make a profound impact.

The three rules of living a fulfilled, purpose-driven life are FAITH, FOCUS, and ACTION. You will need all three in order to fulfill your journey and become who you are meant to be.

You don't have to know all the answers ahead of time, because as Martin Luther King stated, we don't have to see the entire staircase, just take one step at a time. When you do that you WILL reach the top of the staircase and there waiting for you will be the LIFESTYLE you want and DESERVE, for yourself and for your family.

Do you want it for yourself? If so, I want it for you! You can have it. I stand here as an example of what can happen when you believe and you keep climbing that staircase, one step at a time. When you exercise your faith, stay laser focused and take consistent action!

God bless you on your journey to becoming who you are.

About the Author

Chereace A. Richards, a leader in her community and role model for many, lives by a simple, yet complex creed: *Embrace your passion, whatever it may be, and fulfill it no matter the cost. Never be comfortable with simply achieving just the status quo.* Chereace is creating a path guided by faith and focus, and using her success to show others how to reach for, and grasp, all of life's infinite possibilities.

In 2006, Chereace was introduced to 5LINX, a rapidly growing, global telecommunications company. She had no prior direct sales experience, but the opportunity filled a void in her life and forced her to challenge herself like never before. Chereace's success with 5LINX has been constant and rather extraordinary. She and her husband have built a flourishing business that is rewarding on many levels. In just four years, they achieved the top position in the company of Double Platinum Senior Vice President (SVP). The Richards have also consistently ranked #1 as Double Platinum SVPs and their team has regularly placed at the #1 and #2 spots in production, company-wide. Chereace often explains how great it is to be able to "live full-time and work part-time." Chereace's life epitomizes the value of having unwavering dedication to whatever you put your mind to.

She uses her story to empower others, specifically women, to:

1. Have Faith,
2. Focus and
3. Take Action every day on your dreams.

With FAITH, laser FOCUS, and most importantly, **ACTION**, Chereace knows that anything is possible.

Her purpose is to empower women to discover their passion and become all that God created them to be. Chereace believes that women can run a successful business, raise a happy family, and still have time for themselves. Having put her dreams to the side on a few occasions, she is now living a new, re-energized life, one that uses faith, focus, and following through as its foundation.